This book belongs to:

For my sons Jackson and Ashton.

Dream big, my little heroes xxx

Matador
Unit E2 Airfield Business Park,
Harrison Road, Market Harborough,
Leicestershire. LE16 7UL
Tel: 0116 279 2299
Email: books@troubador.co.uk
Web: www.troubador.co.uk/matador
Twitter: @matadorbooks

ISBN 978 1803130 705

British Library Cataloguing in Publication Data.
A catalogue record for this book is available from the British Library.

Typeset in 20pt Noteworthy by Troubador Publishing Ltd, Leicester, UK

Matador is an imprint of Troubador Publishing Ltd

THE Magical Dream Box

LAURA GRAY

ILLUSTRATED BY EMILIA RUMIŃSKA

If ever you feel frightened, close your eyes and you will find your very own Magical Dream Box in the corners of your mind.

Open up your box and discover a glittering invitation,
to do and see all your favourite things just by using your imagination.

Take a walk into the woods,
hear the birds and bumblebees,
play hide and seek with the animals
among the long grass and the trees.

Build a great big tree swing
to fly across a turbulent stream,
then jump off at the other side
like a jungle king or queen.

Break through the undergrowth and
find an edible maze of treats –
cupcakes, jellybeans, chocolate coins –
all just for you to eat.

Then when you reach the middle,
ride a rocket into the sky,
and fly on through a rainbow haze
sparkling way up high.

Take the most enormous jump
and land upon a cloud,
feel your tummy tickle and turn
as you swiftly float on down.

Land into a waterfall to
refresh and jump around,
splish and splash to your heart's content
as the water rushes to the ground.

Dry off at the sunny beach,
building giant castles in the sand,
listen to the sound of the waves
as they crash against the land.

Sit back and admire the sunset in
beautiful oranges, pinks and reds,
watch the water twinkle like the stars
over the deep blue sea ahead.

As night falls, set up for camping and
roast marshmallows around the fire,
dance freely in the moonlight
until you slowly begin to tire.

And when the rain begins to patter,
cuddle up in your cosy tent,
full of sleeping bags and cuddly toys,
feeling calm, relaxed and content.

If you begin to feel afraid
or wake up lonely in the night,
just know you have the power
to make everything alright.

For your wondrous mind has no limits,
it can take you far and wide,
so discover YOUR Magical Dream Box,
lie back and enjoy the ride.

Where will your
Magical Dream
Box take you?

Lightning Source UK Ltd.
Milton Keynes UK
UKHW051858181221
395834UK00005B/54

9 781803 130705